Beaches of Sussex

Emily Broadhurst

First printing: 2015

ISBN-13: 978-1516836833
ISBN-10: 1516836839

For further information, please contact the author at info@beachesofsussex.com or visit the website at www.beachesofsussex.com

DEDICATION

To uber-daddy, my own
personal taxi service,
come rain or shine (but
mostly rain!) I love you
so much and without you
none of this would have
been possible.

INTRODUCTION

Dear Reader,

If you are picking up this book, you are wondering what the beaches of Sussex have to offer you. From bustling cities to quiet, tranquil beaches, this book has everything that you need, with a summary and information on each of the ten beaches that I have chosen to review. These small seaside towns may offer a quiet release from city life, or an opportunity to see Sussex in a new light. This book doesn't have to be read front to back – you can simply flip and flick to the pages which you want to read most. This book will increase your historical knowledge about the beaches in Sussex, as well as helping you and your family know where to go to relax among the picturesque views. I hope you will soon discover the charm of a Sussex beach.

CONT

ENTS

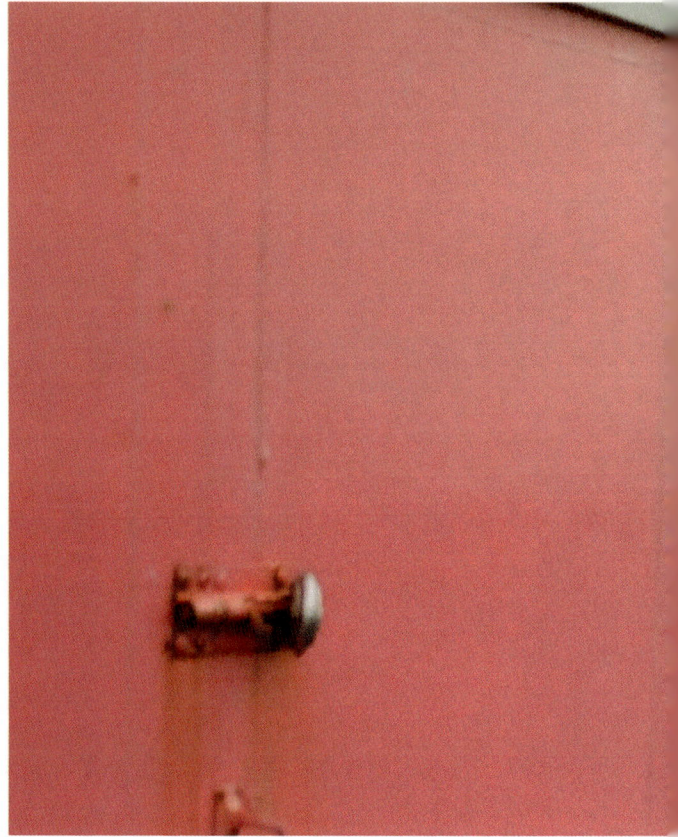

FURTHER INFORMATION

What the Awards mean:

The Marine Conservation Society Recommended (MCS): This is defined by having excellent water quality. But be warned that over 68% of all Britain's beaches have water pollution problems from runoffs from sewers and farms. Beach litter is also taken into consideration.

Blue Flag beach award: This is the best award for beaches and is internationally recognised, with the award being given according to four important factors: environmental education and information, water quality, environmental management, and safety and services (such as available drinking water). The designation of awards is carried out annually, so beaches can either lose or gain the status.

The Quality Coast Award: This is given when a beach is kept continually tidy and includes funding to further improve the beach.

For all beaches, remember to swim close to the shore, don't jump or dive from groynes or other structures. Do not swim after drinking or eating – wait awhile. Remember that the sun is merciless and will give you sun burn, so wear at least factor 15 sun screen. Free sun protection is sometimes available from the lifeguards. Apart from this, sit back, relax and enjoy the sun.

Camber Sands Beach

Nearest town: Rye
County: East Sussex
Postcode: TN31 7RT

"We are ocean. back whether watch – we are going back from whence we came..." – J.F. Kennedy

tied to the
And when we go
to the sea,
it is to sail or to

Camber Sands is a beautiful, sandy beach which emanates a paradisiacal and picturesque feel,making it number one in the list. Camber Sands is located in the small town of Camber, near Rye in East Sussex. It is well known for its prime location for kite surfing, kite landboarding and kitebuggying. But, more importantly,it is known for the long ridges of sand dunes leading to miles of golden sands. It has the only sand dune system in East Sussex which gives a valuable natural habitat to the local wildlife. The famous Camber has been the location for some films, including the award winning the Theory of Everything, as well as others such as Monuments Men and the Invisible Woman.

To travel to this beach by train the nearest stations are Rye and Winchelsea, on the Hastings to Ashford line. There are also a few buses that travel to Camber from Rye, such as the 711 bus straight to Camber, which drops you off just a short walk to the beach. If you are driving you have to take the main A259 coast road through C24 to Camber; from there, you can follow the signs and make your way to the beach. There is a paid car park opposite the beach which closes at 8pm (as does the beach). This car park is pay on entry from Easter to the end of September, and in the winter pay and display machines are used.

For sea safety, red flags mean no swimming and orange mean no inflatables. If you want to have a barbeque, you are allowed. However, there are some rules, which include not using disposable BBQs (gas powered only) and gaining permission from the Neighbourhood Services Office for large numbers of people

(more than ten). Note that it is illegal to BBQ on the sand dunes. Finally, only use the western end of Camber Sands beach for BBQs. At a few times in the year in Camber, in warm weather, jellyfish and weever fish are found in shallow waters. Bathers should be careful in the waters in the summer as these fish can sting. It is good advice to wear footwear during swimming. If you do get stung by a jellyfish, try not to touch the affected area; instead, lightly spray the area with sea water and put ice on it. If you get stung by a weever fish, place the affected area in hot water.

"Writers begin grain of sand, create a

Dogs, although they are restricted, are still allowed to walk on the beach. They are permitted in zoned areas F and H for most of the year – always on a lead – but are not allowed at all in between May and September.

I hope you enjoy this sandy and gorgeous beach. But if your journey doesn't end here, another lovely beach, Broomhill Sands,is just under a mile away.

with a
and then
beach."
– Robert Black

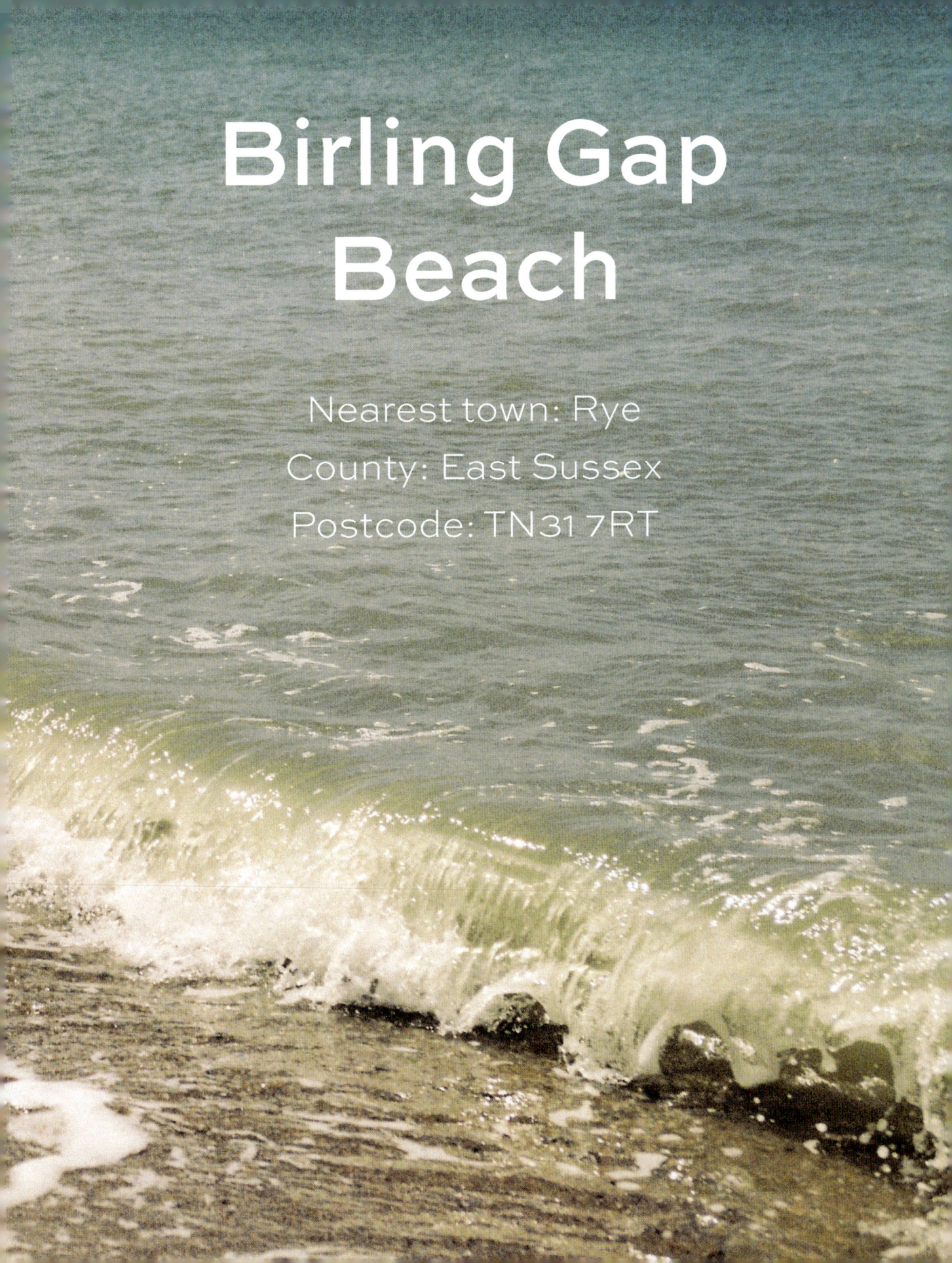

Birling Gap Beach

Nearest town: Rye

County: East Sussex

Postcode: TN31 7RT

"Eternity begins and ends with the ocean's tides." – Unknown

Birling Gap is a narrow, long beach next to beautiful chalk cliffs. Birling gap has an essence of tranquillity that the other beaches don't have – you can sometimes walk along the beach and only see two or three people. However, especially in peak season on weekends, many travel to sit and let the beauty of the cliffs wash over them. Birling Gap is part of the Seven Sisters, which are one of the longest stretches of undevelopedcliffs in the South of England. It is not overlooked. The actual beach is large pebbles with a few patches of sand, all in front of chalk cliffs. The cliffs are eroding, thus the sharp, white colouring, so be careful not to sit too close.

There are many things to do at this beach: you can take long walks across the cliffs, or walk down to the pebble beach which was awarded a Blue Flag in 2005, where you can bask in the glorious views. The beach is also popular for dog walks, cycling, hiking and walking paths, bird watching, swimming and sun bathing. It has excellent water quality and is the proud holder of a Marine Conservation Society recommendation. The National Trust are trying to improve the beach to ensure an even greater day out by developing a garden, a shop, an extension on the café and improvements to the parking.

11

"The sea lives in every one of us." — Wyland

There is parking provided, very close to the beach, and it is advisable to drive to because the nearest train station, Eastbourne, is four miles away.

Be warned that some parts of this beach are open to nudists. However, this is well restricted and the beach maintains a friendly atmosphere. If you are going to the nudist section, turn right at the bottom of the stairs and walk about 500 yards; the further you walk the more deserted and tranquil it becomes. Also, as this beach is close to Brighton, it isoften used by people from there, particularly as it is much nicer than the nudist beach in Brighton (Black Rock Beach), which is unfortunately very close to a main road and is overlooked by bystanders.

Another warning is that some parts of the cliffs are very unstable; thus, remember to keep your distance and not to sit too close.There has recently been significant erosion and so many cliffs are still maintaining their white colouring without any dirt. Rocks have been known to fall off the face so avoid spots where this is likely. There are also some rocks in the water, which are obviously dangerous and can make getting in and out of the water not so easy.

West Wittering Beach

Nearest Town: Chichester
County: West Sussex
Postcode: PO20 8AU

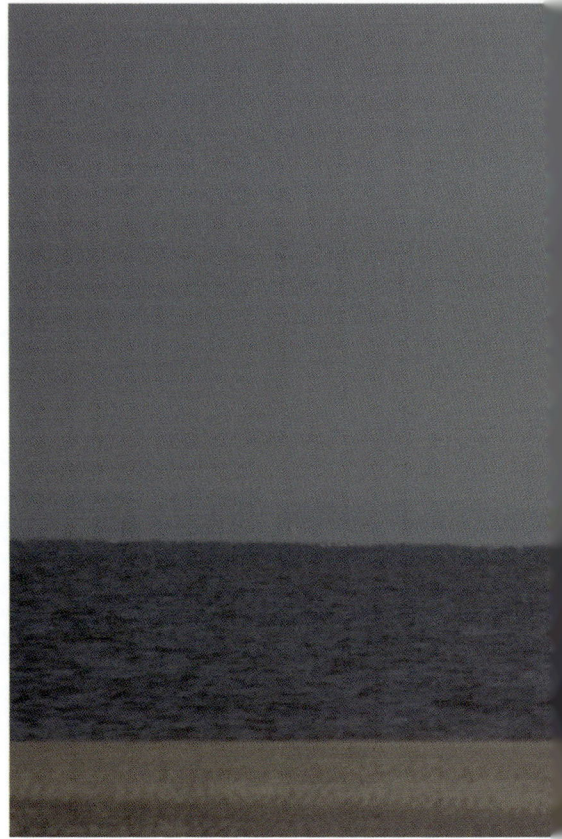

West Wittering is a natural sandy beach which is very popular and considered to be the best beach in West Sussex by many. This is mainly due to its alluring charms and its beautiful nature. It has been depicted as a little piece of heaven and is almost like being abroad. The long stretches of sand are gorgeous. It is internationally recognised for its natural beauty and environment. West Wittering is comprised of large lawns which are perfect for picnicking and barbequing. West Wittering is a clean beach, with little litter, and it has thus become a Blue

Flag Beach, which means it is associated with cleanliness and high standards of safety.

Drivers may choose their parking space from amongst the 20 acres of grass. No part of the lawn is more than 100 yards away from the sandy beach, so you don't have to haul your things very far. The parking charges vary, but be prepared to fork out as much as £8.00 in peak season for parking on a weekend! However, it can drop to as little as £1.00 in low season.

"In every outthrust headland, in every curving beach, in every grain of sand there is the story of the earth." – Rachel Carson

Dogs are prohibited from May to September across the groynes 14a to 18 – this is the area in front of the line of beach huts. However, for the rest of the year you are free to bring your dogs. Owners are responsible for cleaning up their pets: dog bins and bags are located at the beach. But remember to never to leave a dog in a warm car over the summer. From March to October, windsurfing is limited to people who have a West Wittering Windsurf Club membership. Kitesurfing is restricted all year round to WWWC members. Surf board hire and tuition are available. No launching of any motor-powered or sailing dinghies is permitted.

There are plenty of things to do in West Wittering to keep the active entertained, from water sports to golf and local walks. If the weather is not perfect, then maybe you can take a trip to Chichester and enjoy the pleasures of the town. Visit the beautiful Cathedral or the Ox Market Cathedral. Alternatively, you could take the time to investigate what life was like hundreds of years ago in the Fishbourne Roman Palace, or watch a performance at Chichester Festival Theatre. There are many options to enjoy. This beach has many amenities such as a café, toilets, showers and a lost child centre. If you plan to move on to another beach, East Wittering is fairly nearby and is a shingle beach which is just as dazzling as West Wittering.

23

Hastings Beach

Nearest town: Hastings

County: East Sussex

Postcode: TN34 1PF

"On the beach, you can live in bliss." – Dennis Wilson

This is a beach of excellent quality, mostly comprised of heavy stones, with sand being visible at low tide. It has miles of spotless beach with pebbles and sand, and you are a stone's throw away from the town's centre and attractions. Visit this Quality Coast award-winning beach and you are guaranteed to have an amazing day, which will be perfect for the whole family. Pelham beach, in particular, is kid friendly with characters to help children recognise where they are on the beach, to try and battle anyone becoming lost.

Hastings town centre is buzzing with people and is being revived and modernised. It has a shopping focus and has all the big name brands. It is pedestrianised and very easy to navigate around. You will not have trouble parking in Hastings: it has a multi-storey car park, as well as other options nearby. If you want to come by rail, Hastings railway station is less than a mile away. But if you don't want to take the train you can also come by bus. If you're coming from London, because Hastings beach is situated in the South, you make your way on the A21 southwards.

In terms of dogs, there are some dog free areas. Dogs have to be kept on a leash all the time when walking on the promenade. They must also be on a lead at Rock a Nore, which is between Groynes 1 and 3. Dog owners can use the beach from the Pier (Groyne 32 to 42).

Up on the West Hill are the ruins of Hastings castle, built by William the Conqueror straight after the Battle of Hastings in 1066. Visitors explore the ruins whilst enjoying the amazing views of the whole beach from above. Another place to explore is the Hastings Pier, originally built in 1872 by the Earl of Granville. Sadly, the original pier burnt down and a new one was built. During the years it has switched uses: in the 60s to 70s it hosted rock bands;then, in the 80s, it had an under-18s disco;nowadays, it has become a gathering of many different little arts and crafts shops.

Bracklesham Bay

Nearest town: Bracklesham

County: West Sussex

Postcode: PO20 8JS

"Our knowledge is a little island in a great ocean of nonknowledge." – Isaac Bashevis Singer

Bracklesham Bay is a coastal town in West Sussex. It faces the English Channel and, surprisingly, even the Isle of Wight can be seen from the beach. This sandy beach is especially popular with windsurfers, divers and surfers, but more famously with fossil hunters. It is favoured by windsurfers because of its strong winds, due to the beach being affected by the south westerly winds from the English Channel. It is an excellent spot for beginners because it is eight miles of continuous beach, so there is plenty of room for manoeuvres.

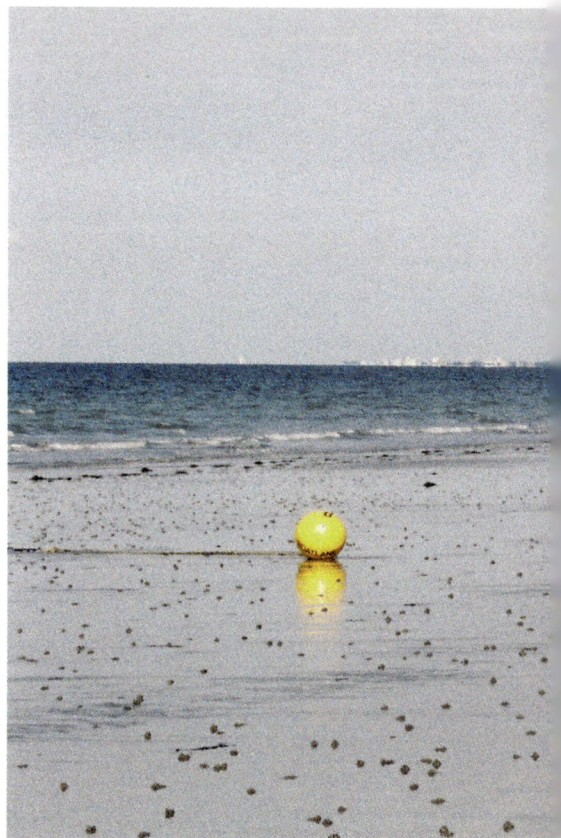

Bracklesham Bay is also well known for its fossil bed, which is visible at low tide. The beds made from clays and marls continue through to Hampshire and then to the Isle of Wight. One is able to collect many things including ray and shark teeth and, more interestingly, bivalve shells. In these beds you can sometimes even find coral. Bracklesham is the perfect place to bring children – you can simply walk along the beach and pick fossils from the

sand. Even if you never find fish remains or teeth you will come away having had an amazing day and with a bag full of striking shells. Remarkably, these fossils date back to approximately forty six million years ago! Recently, however, because the clays are vulnerable to erosion in the fossil bed, a lot of land has been lost. Extensive protection will be needed if the coast is to survive.

"The sea! the sea!, The the ever – Bryan W.

Be warned that in summer there is slow moving traffic because it is a popular family destination.To avoid this, congestion is generally at the start and nearing the end of the day. Even people in London travel down to this location because of its strong winds and it is a form of escapism for them from their busy and stressful London lives. Unhappily, a dog ban is in force and dogs are completely prohibited. But it is still well worth the visit, a fact which is backed up by the Marine Conservation Society Recommendation.

For travel to this beach from Chichester, take the A286 and B2198. The beach is accessible by ramp but also by steps. If you are taking the bus, routes 52 and 53 are applicable. Finally, the nearest train station is Bosham, but this is six miles away so driving is recommended. Parking spaces are plentiful.

sea! the open blue, the fresh, free!." Procter

Brighton Beach

Nearest Town: Brighton

County: East Sussex

Postcode: BN2 1TW

Brighton Beach, famous for its beautiful restored pier, holds both Blue Flag and Quality Coast awards. This beach is very well visited and has great appeal. Expect to join up to 150,000 people or more on a weekend in the summer. It is a bustling beach, filled with all things, for all people, and it is often referred to as "London on the Sea." Brighton itself is a traditional town that thousands flock to during heatwaves, and it is well known for its lively nightlife, having more than 400 pubs. This town promises a great experience for visitors, with the promenade full of up-and-coming and award-winning cafes, restaurants and bars.

"Even the upper end of the river believes in the ocean." – William Stafford

Along the beach, sailing and other water sports are offered. There is also an area devoted to nudist visitors in the eastern part of the promenade. However, it is more overlooked than other beaches and if you are going to use this, I would suggest visiting Birling gap where it is beautiful and much more secluded.

This is a shingle and sand beach, in the centre of everything, the buzz of one of the most quintessential towns in England. It holds a rugged charm, which can only be found in one of the bustle of Brighton. The beach is open all year, but it comes to life in the summer when everyone explores Brighton. Tourists, Londoners and children all pour into Brighton to enjoy the interesting nightlife, the festivals, or just to escape from the pressures of their normal lives.

"Even from sand fall the

If you visit Brighton, there is much to enjoy and explore, particularly along the Pier, which is what the beach is most famous for. The Pier has had millions invested in it to restore its beauty and opulence. It offers traditional food, as well as having two arcades, and is one of the most popular tourist attractions in England. The Pier also hosts summer events and parades, which all benefit from the picturesque view of Brighton. To get to this extraordinary pier, there are links in every direction. From Brighton train station it is just over a mile walk to the beach, or on the bus it is twenty minutes. Be warned that from London Victoria it takes 2 hours and 30 minutes by bus and 1 hour and 30 minutes by car. Enjoy. If you are travelling onwards, other nearby beaches are: Kemp Town Brighton, Brighton Naturist and Hove beach.

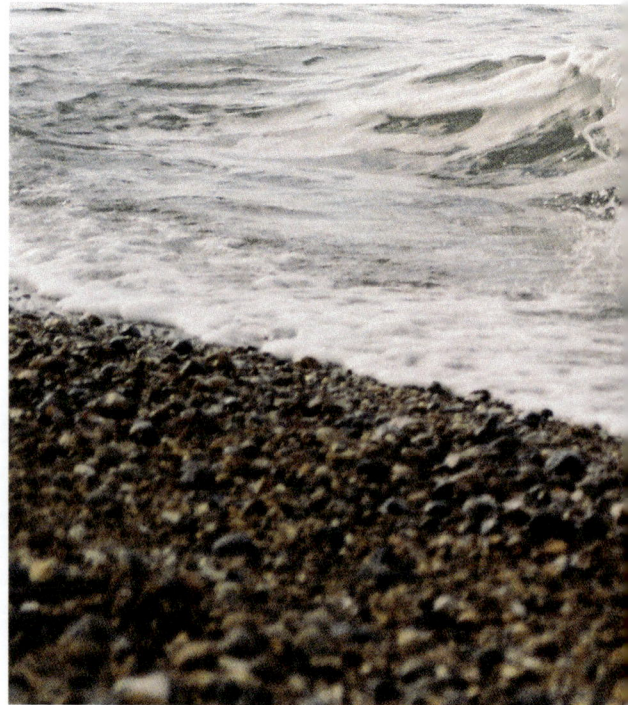

castles made
to
ocean."
– Jimi Hendrix

Bognor Regis Beach

Nearest town: Bognor Regis
County: West Sussex
Postcode: PO21 1JN

This captivating beach is a beautiful shingle beach located in Bognor Regis. Opened in 1865, thousands upon thousands have enjoyed this beach, walking on the beautiful pier structure, indulging in the beach views and relishing the sea air. It is one of the most visited place in Bognor Regis, as many take runs and walk upon the stunning shore.

"Our memories will linger on, footprints in the – Unknown

This is a 2014 Seaside Award beach, with many beachside attractions making it perfect for a family day out. The shingle is very safe for bathing in the summer and is well managed. But be warned that there is no lifeguard service on this beach. Don't worry, though,as this beach is very clean and is maintained on a daily basis in the summer because of the many people that visit it. You could walk, cycle, skate or run down the wide promenade, or give children a ride on the Bognor Regis Promenade Train. If you are sportier, you can sail, kayak, Jet Ski or windsurf with the Bognor Regis Yacht Club and launch it from the Gloucester Road Water Craft Launch Ramp in the summer. At this beach you can party the night away in a night club, game into oblivion in the amusement arcade or just go back to basics and appreciate the sea views. Nearby there are cafes, restaurants and a couple of shops too.

of the ocean long after our sand are gone."

Travelling to this beach should be no problem. The nearest train station is Bognor Regis and is less than a mile away. It is around ten minutes' walk to the beach and there is also a bus service (National Express). Parking is plentiful, and there are many options for short stay and long stay parking in the nearby vicinity.

This beach is dog friendly during off-season, but dogs are banned 1st April to 30th September. It has dog bins and litter bins provided. If this is not the end of the road for you there are some other beaches nearby such as East Bognor Regis, Bognor Regis and Felpham, all around one mile away.

Littlehampton Beach

Nearest town: Littlehampton

County: West Sussex

Post Code: BN16 2NA

"Limitless and immortal, the waters are the beginning and end of all things on earth."
– Heinrich Zimmer

The beach in Littlehampton is a Blue Flag beach. It is great for the family because of its promenade train in the summer, which rides children and parents up and down the length of the promenade.

This shingle and sandy beach is famous for having the longest bench in Britain. This bench stretches most of the length of the beach, snaking around the bushes, ducking into the ground at gates, and around bins. It can accommodate 300 people and stretches 324 metres. It is made from reclaimed wood from old groynes and wood saved from the land fill. In mounting ideas working with a local school to give them insight onto the beach. To help fund the project there are hundreds of engraved personal messages on the bench.

"In one drop of water are found all the secrets of all the oceans." – Kahlil Gibran

One of the most unique and interesting things about Littlehampton beach is the amazing East Beach Café, built by renowned designer Thomas Heatherwick, who you may know as the creator of the 2012 Olympic Cauldron. The café is intriguing from the outside and resembles a cave inside. The food and the structure have a high stamp of approval. The opening was much anticipated by all the locals and internationally also, featuring all across the world in the news, including Vogue Japan and the New York Times. However, if looking at the promenade is not your thing then you can make your way over to West Beach Café and enjoy looking at the sand dunes and the beach. Be sure to check it out as it was named one of Times' 20 best places to eat by the beach 2013. Don't worry about parking as there are plenty of places to park from behind East Beach Café to next to the playground for little kids.

Pevensey Bay

Nearest town: Eastbourne

County: East Sussex

Postcode: BN24 6HX

"Don't grow up lest you you love the

This shingle beach located in the town of Pevensey and holds the Marine Conservation Society award. Be careful to take note of the rules, however, because dogs are restricted to certain areas on this beach.

Pevensey is a village and a parish in East Sussex, England. The main village is 5 miles north east of Eastbourne. It is most widely known for the fact that it was here that William the Conqueror first landed and invaded the country in 1066. This was after crossing the English Channel from France. This small village was founded in the 1600s and is an old fishing town. Today, however, it is a popular tourist town with historic Pevensey castle nearby.

too quickly,
forget how much
beach."
– Michelle Held

The Pevensey Bay Sailing Club offers many different types of boats, but you have to be a member to take advantage of this. Visit their website for more details http://www.pbsc.eu/about-us/join-our-club/. Pevensey is the perfect place

to go kayaking or canoeing; it is also a tranquil spot for fishing. Nearby are cafés and restaurants with disabled facilities. Pevensey bay is known for its fishing and its historic Martello Towers. These towers were used for Napoleonic defence in the 1800s.

the sea is sensuous, enfolding the body in its soft, close embrace."
– Kate Chopin

"The voice of the sea speaks to the soul. The touch of

To get to this beach, the nearest train station is Pevensey Bay with which is around one mile away. Pevensey and Westham station also serves this area but is further away. To drive from the A27 between Eastbourne and Bexhill, turn off in Pevensey and follow the signs to the bay and beach. If, however, you are coming from Eastbourne town centre, follow the A259 North East along the coast and you will reach Pevensey bay. If you are coming from anywhere else, you should enter the postcode into the SAT-NAV to find Pevensey. Don't worry about parking – it is nearby and fairly spacious.

West Quay Beach

Nearest town: Newhaven

County: East Sussex

Postcode: BN9 9HD

"For whatever we lose (like a you or a me), It's always our self we find in the sea" – E.E.Cummings

Located in East Sussex, this beach is all shingle and sand. Against the backdrop of amazing cliffs, you can enjoy the gorgeous scenery as well as the activities and facilities which this beach offers. At the top of the cliffs are some tunnels which lead straight to the beach, making this beach the perfect place for children to explore and play in. This beach appeals to most as dogs are allowed, but there are no dog bins. It is Marine Conservation Society Recommended as well as being popular with the locals in the summer.

There is much to explore in West Quay including the historical Newhaven Fort, originally built for the defence of the south coast harbour which is in Newhaven. Built in 1859, it is now the largest defence project in Sussex and is used as a museum. If you are interested in the history of Newhaven, try visiting the Newhaven Museum which is extremely well informed on all aspects of Newhaven over the years,including smuggling, celebrations, famous people, the harbour and much more. It is located in Paradise Family Leisure Park on Avis Road. If you like the outdoors, activities such as snorkelling, swimming, boating, canoeing, scuba diving, jetskiing and diving are all available. There are opportunities to enjoy all the facilities. But be warned that there is no lifeguard and you should keep an eye on all children.

"The cure for anything is salt water – sweat, tears, or the sea."
– Isak Dinesen

To get to this stunning beach, the best access point is from Newhaven town centre: from South Way, turn left to Riverside and then left again at Fort Road, which leads to the carpark for the beach. The nearest train station is Newhaven Town, which is just under one mile away and is fifteen minutes' walk away from the beach. For parking, the nearest car park is right next to the beach and is made extremely convenient.

If your journey does not end here, Newhaven beach is walking distance from West Quay,another beautiful shingle beach in the same town. In the distance is Seaford Bay and Dane if you are willing to go further for a change of scenery.

ABOUT THE AUTHOR

My name is Emily Broadhurst and I am aged 15. I attend a local school and I have always been passionate about the beach. After visiting beaches around Sussex, I decided to take my knowledge of the beaches and turn it into a book. I live near the beach and my earliest childhood memories are of visiting the beach with my mum and sister. Each year, we add to our family shell jars and they are now overflowing with beautiful shells, from odd rocks to big clam shells.

17372008R00054

Printed in Great Britain
by Amazon